THE LIZARD LIBRARY™

The Komodo Dragon

Jake Miller

The Rosen Publishing Group's
PowerKids Press™
New York

Published in 2003 by The Rosen Publishing Group, Inc.
29 East 21st Street, New York, NY 10010

First Edition

Editor: Nancy MacDonell Smith
Book Design: Maria E. Melendez
Book Layout: Eric DePalo

Photo Credits: Cover and title page, 17, 20, 22 © Wolfgang Kaehler/CORBIS; p. 4 © Glenn Vanstrum/Animals Animals; p. 7 © Jodi Jacobson/Peter Arnold, Inc.; pp. 8, 19 © Roland Seitre/Peter Arnold, Inc.; p. 11 © Compost/Visage/BIOS/Peter Arnold, Inc.; pp. 12, 13 © Michael K. Nichols, National Geographic Image Collection; p. 14 © Roman Soumar/CORBIS; p. 15 © Fred Bruemmer/Peter Arnold, Inc.; p. 16 © Bob Krist/CORBIS.

Miller, Jake, 1969–
The Komodo dragon / Jake Miller.
    p.   cm. — (The lizard library)
Includes bibliographical references.
Summary: This book introduces the life cycle and habits of the komodo dragon.
    ISBN 0-8239-6416-7 (lib.)
1. Komodo dragon—Juvenile literature   [1. Komodo dragon   2. Lizards]   I. Title   II. Series
    QL666.L29 M56 2003
    597.95'968—dc21

                                                                                    2001-007769

Manufactured in the United States of America

Contents

Komodo dragons have bright yellow tongues.

The World's Largest Lizard

Komodo dragons are the biggest lizards in the world. They often grow to be between 8 and 10 feet (2.5–3 m) long from nose to tail. They have big, flat heads, strong legs, and long, thick bodies. Adult Komodos are a dull gray color. Male Komodo dragons are bigger than females. The biggest males can grow to be 11 feet (3.35 m) long. That's as long as two grown-ups lying end to end. A big male Komodo can weigh as much as 550 pounds (249 kg). It is easy to see why some people might think that Komodos look like dragons. They are big, with a lot of sharp teeth. When a Komodo **flicks** out its long, forked tongue, it almost looks like it is breathing fire. Just like dragons in fairy tales, Komodos are very dangerous. They will eat any animal into which they can get their teeth. Komodos even eat each other!

5

Discovering the Dragons

You would think that it would be pretty hard to miss such a big, scary lizard, but scientists only found out about Komodo dragons in 1912, less than 100 years ago. The Komodo dragon lives on the islands of Komodo, Rintja, Padar, Flores, and a handful of other small islands in the Flores Sea. These islands are part of Indonesia, a country south of Asia, in the Indian Ocean. These islands were very far from the big cities where scientists lived. The people who lived on the islands knew about the giant lizards for hundreds of years. They told travelers stories about the giant lizards, but no one believed the stories. When scientists started traveling to the small islands, they learned that Komodos were real and not just **legends**.

Komodo dragons spend most of their time alone, searching for food. They eat goats, pigs, and deer.

6

Once upon a Time

The **ancestors** of Komodo dragons were probably smaller lizards that came to the islands from Australia more than a million years ago. These smaller lizards made the trip during a long-ago **ice age**. During an ice age, much of the world's water is frozen solid. This means that even in warm parts of the world, there is less water in the oceans. Less water made it easier for the lizards to swim from island to island. When the ice melted, the waters of the ocean rose, and the islands were **isolated**. The lizards were left on the island without any other major **predators**. There were a lot of big animals for them to eat, including a **species** of small elephants. The lizards **evolved** over time. They grew bigger and stronger until they were the perfect elephant eaters. Today the small elephants are **extinct**.

Komodo dragons are very strong swimmers, even though they spend most of their time on land.

A Day in the Life of a Dragon

Although they are in the middle of the ocean, the Flores Islands are dry. The islands are covered with grasslands and forests. Most of the year it doesn't rain at all on the islands. The weather is very hot. The coolest it gets is 63°F (17°C), and it often gets up to 109°F (43°C). Komodo dragons sleep in the cool air of the night and are active during the day. Komodos are **cold-blooded**. In the morning, they sit in the sun to warm up. Then they spend a few hours looking for food. When it gets very hot, Komodos rest in **burrows** or under a shady tree. If the afternoon is cool enough, the dragons go back out again to look for more food. Komodos can go without water for days, but if they are thirsty they will gulp down gallons (l) of water at a time.

Komodos usually dig their own burrows, but they also take over burrows from other animals, such as porcupines.

10

Komodos have powerful jaws and 57 very sharp teeth. A Komodo uses its tail to knock over its prey. Then the Komodo uses its teeth to tear apart the prey.

Born to Bite and Fight

Komodos are members of a **family** of lizards called **monitors**. Monitors are all expert predators. Komodos are huge and very strong. They often fight with each other. They don't like to share their food. Sometimes a big Komodo will try to eat a smaller Komodo. They can run 11 miles per hour (18 km/h) for short periods of time. On top of all of that, Komodos are some of the smartest lizards in the world, so they know just how to use their strength, their speed, and their size. For example, they learn all the paths on which animals like to walk, and wait there for just the right moment to attack.

When a Komodo dragon's teeth wear out, new ones grow in. A Komodo can grow 200 new teeth in a year.

13

Dinnertime

Komodos eat all types of small animals, even monkeys. When a Komodo dragon is hunting, it hides near a path that animals use to walk through the grass or the woods. The Komodo waits for an animal to pass by, then jumps out and bites the animal. The Komodo dragon's **saliva** contains several types of **bacteria**. When a dragon bites an animal, the bacteria make the animal sick. If the dragon doesn't kill the animal right away, it is easy for the dragon to catch and eat the weakened animal. Dragons also eat any dead animals that they can find. They can smell a **carcass** from 7 miles (11 km) away and will go to find it.

A scientist once saw a Komodo eat a 90-pound (41-kg) pig in 17 minutes!

This Komodo dragon will use its teeth to tear off chunks of the deer's flesh and bones. Komodos swallow without chewing.

Komodo dragons have to be careful when they choose a place to leave their eggs because other Komodo dragons will eat the eggs if they find them.

Dragon Eggs

When a female Komodo is ready to have babies, she digs a *U*-shaped burrow in sandy soil. The dragon lays from 1 to 30 eggs in the bottom of the burrow. Female dragons lay their eggs only once a year, usually in August or September. Komodo parents don't stay near the eggs once they are laid, and they don't take care of their young once they **hatch**. The eggs are smooth and soft, not like the eggs you get at the supermarket. The eggs are between 2 ½ and 4 ½ inches (6–11 cm) long. The young Komodo dragons hatch after eight or nine months, at the end of the islands' short rainy season. This way there is plenty of water for the young Komodos when they are born.

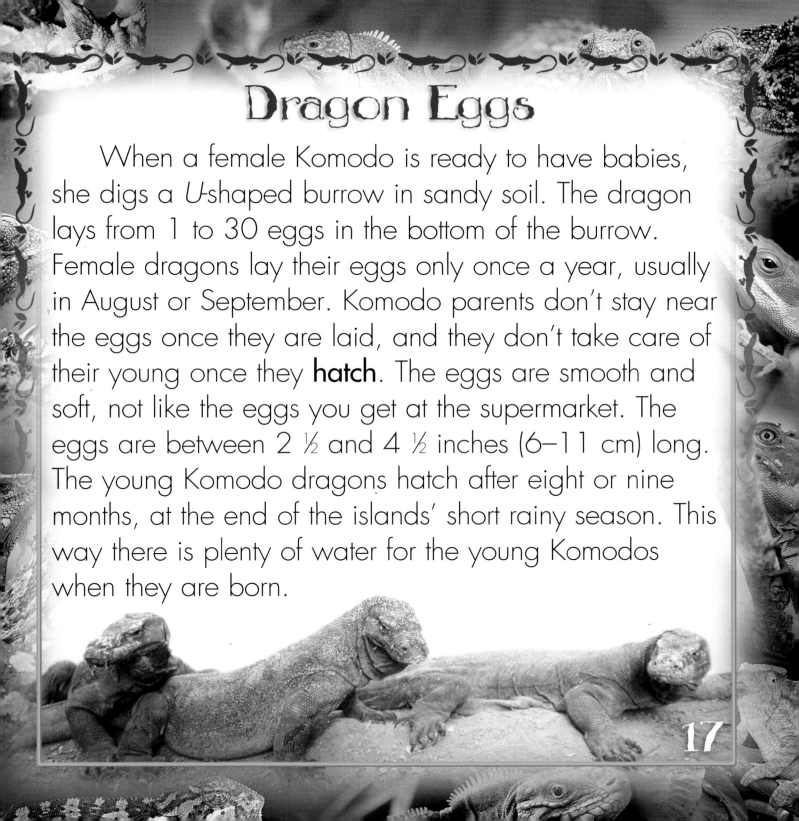

17

Growing Up

When they hatch, baby Komodos are from 8 to 22 inches (20–56 cm) long. The babies grow very quickly. Between the time they are born and the time they're a year and a half old, Komodos nearly double in size. Adult Komodo dragons continue to grow, but much more slowly. Some Komodo dragons may live to be 50 years old. Young dragons look so different from adults that they seem to be a different species. Instead of being a dull gray color, young Komodos are bright green with black stripes and red circles. They spend most of their time in trees. Young Komodos eat insects, lizards, rats, birds, snakes, and other animals that they hunt in the trees. If they were on the ground, the young dragons would be in danger of being eaten by larger dragons. By the time they are too big to stay up in the

Komodo dragons continue to grow for their whole lives. The biggest one on record was 10 feet 4 inches (3 m) long.

treetops, young Komodos are big enough to protect themselves from adult Komodos.

Living with Dragons

Komodos spend most of their time alone. However, if one Komodo kills an animal or finds a dead one, many other Komodos may come to join the feast. If the animal isn't big enough to feed all the Komodos, or if one of the Komodos is much bigger than the others, the dragons may fight. Komodos also have to live with many other kinds of animals. Dogs, birds, snakes, and wild cats will all attack and eat young dragons if they have the chance. Sometimes dogs will try to steal food from Komodo dragons. Komodos also share their islands with humans. Komodos will attack a person if he is not paying attention or is weak or sick. Komodos like to attack things that are easy to kill. If you try to scare a dragon off with a stick, it will usually leave you alone. Still, it's best to stay far away from Komodo dragons.

 A group feast, like this one, is one of the few times when a Komodo dragon will spend time with other Komodos.

Dragons at the Zoo

Since there are fewer than 5,000 Komodos in the world, it is important to protect them. Indonesia has set up several parks where no one is allowed to kill or to capture a Komodo. Zoos around the world are learning how to take care of Komodo dragons so that they never become extinct.

Some Komodo dragons in zoos seem to become tame. They will drink water out of their keepers' hands and come when their keepers whistle for them. However, Komodo dragons are still dangerous, wild animals that must always be treated with respect.

The dull color of this Komodo's skin means it is fully grown.

Glossary

ancestors (AN-ses-turz) Animals, plants, or people that were alive long ago that gave rise to the things and people living today.

bacteria (bak-TEER-ee-uh) Tiny living things that can only be seen with a microscope.

burrows (BUR-ohz) Holes that animals dig in the ground for shelter.

carcass (KAR-kus) The body of a dead animal.

cold-blooded (KOHLD-bluh-did) Having a body temperature that changes with the surrounding temperature.

evolved (ee-VOLVD) Changed or developed over many years.

extinct (ik-STINKT) No longer existing.

family (FAM-lee) The scientific name for a large group of plants or animals that are alike in some ways.

flicks (FLIKS) Moves quickly and suddenly.

hatch (HACH) To come out of an egg.

ice age (EYES AYJ) A period of time when ice and glaciers covered parts of the land.

isolated (EYE-suh-layt-ed) Separate from other things.

legends (LEH-jendz) Stories that people tell that may not be true.

monitors (MAH-nuh-turz) A family of lizards that includes the Komodo dragon.

predators (PREH-duh-terz) Animals that kill other animals for food.

saliva (suh-LY-vuh) The liquid in the mouth that starts to break down food and helps food to slide down the throat.

species (SPEE-sheez) A single kind of plant or animal. For example, all people are one species.

Index

Web Sites

Due to the changing nature of Internet links, PowerKids Press has developed an online list of Web sites related to the subject of this book. This site is updated regularly. Please use this link to access the list: www.powerkidslinks.com/ll/komodrag/